THE POWER OF PODCASTING

Maximize Your Impact and Income

> **Special FREE Bonus Gift for You**
>
> To help you to achieve more success in your business, there are **FREE BONUS RESOURCES** for you at:
>
> ### FreeGiftFromNick.com
>
> - Three in depth videos on how to grow your business through content creation, and re-purposing
> - Downloadable "Roadmap to Podcasting" Resource Guide

NICK PALKOWSKI
Your Podcast Guru

Copyright 2015 by Nick Palkowski

ALL RIGHTS RESERVED. No part of this book or its associated ancillary materials may be reproduced or transmitted in any form or by any means, electronic or mechanical, including photocopying, recording, or by any informational storage or retrieval system without permission from the publisher.

PUBLISHED BY: Your Podcast Guru.

DISCLAIMER AND/OR LEGAL NOTICES

While all attempts have been made to verify information provided in this book and its ancillary materials, neither the author or publisher assumes any responsibility for errors, inaccuracies or omissions and is not responsible for any financial loss by customer in any manner. Any slights of people or organizations are unintentional. If advice concerning legal, financial, accounting or related matters is needed, the services of a qualified professional should be sought. This book and its associated ancillary materials, including verbal and written training, is not intended for use as a source of legal, financial or accounting advice. You should be aware of the various laws governing business transactions or other business practices in your particular geographical locations.

EARNINGS & INCOME DISCLAIMER

With respect to the reliability, accuracy, timeliness, usefulness, adequacy, completeness, and/or suitability of information provided in this book, Nick Palkowski, Your Podcast Guru, its partners, associates, affiliates, consultants, and/or presenters make no warranties, guarantees, representations, or claims of any kind. Readers' results will vary depending on a number of factors. Any and all claims or representations as to income earnings are not to be considered as average earnings. Testimonials are not representative. This book and all products and services are for educational and informational purposes only. Use caution and see the advice of qualified professionals. Check with your accountant, attorney or professional advisor before acting on this or any information. You agree that Nick Palkowski and/or Your Podcast Guru is not responsible for the success or failure of your personal, business, health, or financial decisions relating any information presented by Nick Palkowski, Your Podcast Guru, or company products/services. Earnings potential is entirely dependent on the efforts, skills and application of the individual person.

Any examples, stories, references, or case studies are for illustrative purposes only and should not be interpreted as testimonies and/or examples of what reader and/or consumers can generally expect from the information. No representation in any part of this information, materials and/or seminar trainings are guarantees or promises for actual performance. Any statements, strategies, concepts, techniques, exercises and ideas in the information, materials and/or seminar training offered are simply opinion or experience, and thus should not be misinterpreted as promises, typical results or guarantees (expressed or implied). The author and publisher (Nick Palkowski, Your Podcast Guru (YPG) or any of YPG's representatives) shall in no way, under any circumstances, be held liable to any party (or third party) for any direct, indirect, punitive, special, incidental or other consequential damages arising directly or indirectly from any use of books, materials and or seminar trainings, which is provided "as is," and without warranties.

This title may be purchased in bulk for educational, business, fund-raising, or sales promotional use. For information, please email, press@YourPodcastGuru.com.

WHAT OTHERS ARE SAYING ABOUT NICK PALKOWSKI & HIS STRATEGIES

I'm so glad I found Nick Palkowski. He's masterful at all things podcasting and he's fantastic to work with! Nick has not only helped me to hit to the top of the charts on iTunes but he's also helped me to stay in my sweet spot! He'll help you to do more of what you do best, help you to grow your audience and help you to have more fun in the process!

- **Mitch Matthews**,
Author, Keynote Speaker, and Podcaster

When I wanted to launch a podcast, I knew I needed all the help I could get. Nick is a really great resource for any questions I have regarding a successful podcast launch, podcast marketing, and he understands the podcasting landscape like no one else I ever met.

- **Joe Apfelbaum**
CEO of Ajax Union

"Nick Palkowski took my 'Achieve Your Goals' podcast from 5,000 downloads (on iTunes) to over 40,000 downloads in the first three months! He is brilliant at what he does, and most importantly, he does EVERYTHING related to publishing a top podcast. I don't know what I'd do without him, and if you'd like to expand your business and grow your brand/influence, don't wait another day to work with Nick!"

- **Hal Elrod**
Author of *The Miracle Morning*

DEDICATION

This book is dedicated to those who are committed to sharing their message, story, and insight with others, and in doing so, they leave the world a bit better than they found it.

And to Julia, who has made my world better since the day we met.

TABLE OF CONTENTS

Introduction...	1
THE WHY	
Adding Value..	7
Starting Your Journey............................	17
THE BASICS	
What is Podcasting...............................	23
A Place to Call Home...........................	43
How to Differentiate Yourself.................	61
THE CONTENT	
What to Talk About...............................	83
Your First Episode.................................	94
THE FUNNEL	
The Funnel Philosophy..........................	109
Launching Your Podcast........................	122
The Future of Podcasts.........................	144
Appendix...	149
Special FREE Gift from Nick.................	161
Additional Resources (Podcasting Services)..	163

THE IDEAL PROFESSIONAL SPEAKER FOR YOUR NEXT EVENT!

Any organization that wants to help their people take their business to the next level, needs to hire Nick for a keynote and/or workshop training

TO CONTACT OR BOOK NICK TO SPEAK:

(507) 459-6293
Nick@YourPodcastGuru.com
YourPodcastGuru.com

MOTIVATE AND INSPIRE OTHERS!
"Share This Book"

Retail $24.95

5-20 Books	$21.95
21-99 Books	$18.95
100-499 Books	$15.95
500-999 Books	$10.95
1,000+ Books	$8.95

To Place an Order Contact:
(507) 459-6293
Nick@YourPodcastGuru.com
YourPodcastGuru.com

WHEN I WAS 6 YEARS OLD I HAD A DREAM...

It's been a crazy road, and I never would have thought I'd end up here. I started *Your Podcast Guru* in a very unexpected way, but it's been one of the best decisions I have ever made.

I've always had a dream of owning my own company, and you can make the claim that I have been on this path for a long time. It all started back in kindergarten — yes, kindergarten. Every day I used to take a sack lunch to school, packed with all kinds of goodies. While I would eat the main meal, I would save some of my snacks, especially the Scooby-Doo gummies; everyone loved those. On the bus ride home I would trade those snacks with some of the other kids for little toys. It started out as small little Happy Meal style toys, but soon I started trading some of those little toys for bigger ones, until eventually I traded all the way up to a bike! The kid's parents were not too happy that their son traded a bike for a handful of toys, and thus my first entrepreneurial venture came to a close … but it was now in my blood.

A few years went by; I was a sophomore in high school. Our school board made the decision to shut down the vending machines during school hours. Being that I was often bored during class, I noticed that in almost every class period about half the class had a soda bottle sitting on their desk. Now they would no longer be able to get those during the day! It just so happened that year I had an empty locker next to mine. After the school board decision, I showed up the next morning with some Styrofoam, ice, and a 24-pack of Mountain Dew. I lined the locker with Styrofoam to create a makeshift cooler, and between class periods I'd sell cans for $1. I was sold out by 11 a.m. That little opportunity lasted a whole two weeks before I showed up to school to find a padlock on the locker next to mine.

PowerOfPodcastingBook.com

The Power of Podcasting

THE WHY

PowerOfPodcastingBook.com

ADDING VALUE

The best way to grow your business is by consistently adding value to your audience.

What are you doing to help your customers … before they are your customers? The tide is starting to really turn. No longer can you just create "brand awareness" or simply try to get your name out there. Now you need to do some real work to add value: you need to teach, educate, and inform your potential clients before they will even consider working with you.

THE FUNNEL PHILOSOPHY

Let me make something very clear up front, **a podcast is not a business**. A podcast is a business asset, a business tool. It's a system to create connections and spread your message in a way that can ultimately lead to profits; but simply releasing podcast episodes on a regular basis does not mean you have a business.

With that out of the way, how can you use a podcast to create profits?

There are multiple ways to monetize a podcast including affiliates, sponsorships, and even having people pay to receive your podcast. I don't focus on any of those. They might be a nice side revenue source, but the way to **grow your business** is by selling your products and services.

Imagine a funnel, like the one my dad taught me to use as a kid when changing the oil on the tractors he used to fix in our garage, one with a big wide end at the top that narrows down to a small opening.

Your business should operate like a funnel. The top of the funnel is where you first bring people into your business. This is where they learn about what you do, where they begin to build an affinity for you. Here's where you focus on building initial relationships with your audience.

As you move down the funnel, the level of affinity, connection, and relationship increases. The amount of money your audience spends on your business also increases. Your ultimate goal is to move people down your funnel.

Podcasting is a top of the funnel activity, it's how you build the initial relationships. It might be the very first interaction people have with you, or at least one of the firsts. Your focus is on providing incredible value for free. It's a focus on serving.

The amount of time someone stays in the top of your funnel varies drastically, but the nice thing about podcasting is they could stay in that part of the funnel for years before they are ready to move down your funnel and because of the way they are set up to scale, it's easy for you to serve them.

EASIEST TO CONSUME

This may come as a surprise to you, especially from someone who started a company called Your Podcast Guru, but I'm not super passionate about podcasts. Yes, I enjoy podcasts and love listening to them, but are they my be-all end-all? No.

What I am super passionate about is helping others grow their businesses by adding value to their audiences on a consistent basis. I believe that is the fundamental way to grow your audience, and podcasting is the best way to do just that.

Podcasting is an amazing tool to add value to your audience because it is the easiest format to consume.

Podcasts are portable. Once downloaded on your phone you don't even need Wi-Fi or a cell signal to play an episode.

They don't require any screen time, making them the perfect medium to consume while driving, working out, or doing the dishes.

Podcasts truly are the most versatile content consumption platform.

CASE STUDY

Hal Elrod The Power of Podcasting

I recently gave a talk at an event that I was at called *Beyond the Bestseller: How to Write a Book that Creates a Movement*, and one of the things I talked about is that you've got to start building your tribe, building your audience right away. The way that I did that is I created an opt-in page at MiracleMorning.com. So if you want to go see how I do this, go to MiracleMorning.com. People put in their name and email address in order to get the first few chapters of the book for free. They get an audio training for free and free video training. All of that at MiracleMorning.com. That's a way where it's automatically adding value to them every time they opt-in. In the book, there's also a site where people can go get a bunch of bonuses. They opt-in, but it's all automated, right? So I don't have to be there to do it. It sends them value.

Now here was the biggest problem. I wasn't adding value consistently to my audience. I was the worst. At the time that Nick and I met, I think I had probably 10,000 people on my email community, on my email list. I would email them once every few months and it was usually the horrible, the worst approach too… when I needed something. Like, "Hey guys. I have my book coming out," great right? It's like, "Hey. Nice Hal. I haven't heard from you in like three months. And of course when I hear from you, it's because you're selling me something. Cool." So it's horrible.

When Nick reached out to me, we talked about this, He said, "What if we did a podcast where all you have to do is show up once a week and record for 30 minutes? Just talk on a microphone for 30 minutes and I'll take care of the rest. All of your email list will get an email every week with value from you. You're not selling them anything. You're just teaching and they're getting to hear your voice. They're getting value directly from you. So now they're going to like you better. They're going to trust you more, right? They're going to have a relationship with you because you're adding value and they're getting to hear your voice and connect with you. That's what got me excited about podcasting and I thought, "Wow. All I have to do is show up for half an hour a week and my audience will get the value that I've been kicking myself for not delivering."

Because writing . . . yes, I'm a writer, I'm an author, but it's more challenging for me. Talking is easier than writing. I'll spend hours on a paragraph or a small blog and then I won't' like it. I will just throw the whole thing away. So the audio's been huge and the podcast's been huge.

But here's the other thing when we launched the podcast, the first month we had 5,000 downloads. That basically means of the 10,000 people in my email community, 5,000 of them were like, "Yeah, I'll check out the podcast."

Month two, we had 7,000 check out the podcast. That basically meant that a few more people decided to pick it up. But here's where it went crazy. Month three we had 27,000 downloads to the podcast. Now you might wonder, "If your email community was only 10,000, how could you have 27,000 downloads? Did your email community explode overnight?" The answer is no. Nick and his ninja strategies, got it noticed on iTunes in the New and Noteworthy sections. There's something on iTunes called New and Noteworthy where the podcasts get featured if you understand how iTunes works their algorithms, which Nick understands that. So it wasn't that my community grew. Well, it did after the fact, but it was because iTunes put up my podcast in their New and Noteworthy and said, "Hey, check this out." Now the millions of people on iTunes that were in the podcast saw my podcast and an extra 20,000 of them or whatever it was decided to listen to it. It really spread organically through iTunes and that was leveraging their audience to grow mine. That's a really powerful aspect of podcasting as well.

STARTING YOUR JOURNEY ...

The time to grab a map is before you enter the woods.

I want to give you a roadmap of how a podcast can fit in your overall business and help create a stronger connection with your customers, ultimately leading to a great lifetime value.

I do not want to help you create a podcast that is in itself your business. That would only be a distraction, merely giving you a platform that is shaky at best and leaves a lot off the table.

You might consider this blasphemy, since this is a book on podcasting, and I run a business called Your Podcast Guru. But what I am most passionate about is growing businesses.

I am a diligent student of marketing and believe in direct response and relationship marketing. I believe that the best way to grow a business is to provide your potential audience with an incredible amount of value to continue to serve them on a repeated, regular, consistent basis; developing that relationship with them over time before going in for the big ask. Podcasting is the best tool I've found for developing that relationship.

In these roadmap sections, I will give you the map to help you along your path. There will be exercises and steps for you to take. Yes, you can skip over these and keep reading, but these are the exact actions I go through with all my podcasting and coaching clients. I strongly suggest you follow this map to get you started. Once you know how to get where you want to go, then feel free to take a more scenic route.

The Power of Podcasting

THE BASICS

PowerOfPodcastingBook.com

WHAT IS PODCASTING?

Podcasting is becoming more and more popular. It's beginning to make its way into the mass market. But there are still many who have no idea what a podcast is. Here's the fastest explanation: a podcast is essentially an on-demand talk-radio show that is delivered directly to you when a new episode is released.

Specifically, in this book we will talk about audio podcasts, but technically speaking podcasts can be in any media format from audio to video to PDFs. What makes podcasts unique from a technical side is that people can subscribe to have updates delivered to them.

When most people think of podcasts they will think of audio podcasts from iTunes. iTunes is one of many directories from which podcasts are available, and we will go into detail on what a directory actually is in a later section. In short, directories are search engines for finding and subscribing to podcasts.

Podcasts are now available on many different devices, from streaming on websites to phones to downloading onto MP3 players. Over 65% of all podcasts are listened to on a mobile device, which is something to keep in mind when creating your content and branding. You still need a high quality website, but more than ever you should tailor the look and feel of your podcast for mobile listeners.

There are many different applications that allow you to subscribe to podcasts, with the biggest being Stitcher and the native Podcast app for iTunes. With these apps people are able to search for shows based on topics they want to hear about and subscribe to them. Once you are subscribed to a podcast, you will be notified each time a new episode is released. You then have the choice to download the episode to listen to later or to stream the content without downloading it. The way I listen to a podcast is by bulk downloading the new episodes when my iPhone is connected to Wi-Fi, so I can listen when I am traveling or working out. I download them on Wi-Fi so I don't have to use up my data plan by downloading or streaming through my cell signal.

Now that we have an overview of what a podcast is, it's time to dive in for a closer look at the process to help you as a future podcaster understand how all the pieces fit together.

A podcast, on a technical side is a media file that is delivered over an RSS (Real Simple Syndication) feed. This is the same type of feed you generate from a blog post, but the difference with a podcast is you place an audio file within the blog post. That means in order to have a podcast you need to have an RSS feed. As someone looking to use your podcast to grow your business, your RSS feed needs to come from a website (there are ways to create an RSS feed without your own self-hosted website, but we will not cover those as it is counterintuitive to the focus of this book).

On your website you will need a blog section. Once you have an audio file ready to be released, you then create a blog post (in the podcasting world this blog post is referred to as your show notes page). Your audio file is then placed into that blog post — with the help of a media host — and then you hit publish. Once you publish the blog post, you are simultaneously creating an RSS feed. iTunes reads your RSS feed (after you submitted your show for approval) and then sends your new episode out to all your subscribers. That, in general, is how a podcast works.

Now that you understand it on a general level, it is time to dive into everything you need to get your podcast up and running.

EQUIPMENT

When talking to people about podcasting, inevitably one of the first questions that comes up is, "*What equipment do I need?*" The truth is, very little. A computer or a smartphone that can record audio is the only essential requirement. If you are podcasting as a hobby that is all you need; don't worry about an extra mic or any other fancy equipment.

However, if this podcast is a business tool, don't settle for second best. The sound quality of a podcast that was recorded with the built-in mic on a computer or (please, no) on a teleconference line is crap compared to one recorded with more sophisticated equipment.

Will the price tag of your podcasting equipment break the bank? No, it doesn't need to. You can spend thousands of dollars on equipment (my home studio cost over $1,000), but the equipment listed below will only cost $120— not bad for a business investment! If that's out of your budget, then podcasting should not be your main focus (harsh, but true).

What do you need to get started?

Now that you are convinced of the importance of investing some money into your podcasting equipment, what do you need to get quality audio? The equipment listed below will get you a great-sounding podcast. If you rate audio on a 0-10 scale, the equipment listed here will have you at an 8. An amazing bargain.

For a complete list of my latest recommended equipment go to YourPodcastGuru.com/BookResources

MICROPHONES

The best microphone to purchase can be a bit of a controversial topic. Once you get involved in microphones and begin noticing some of the nuances, people can take their recommendations a little personally. That's because the best microphone for your voice may not be the best microphone for another person's voice. In the list below I tried to give you some of the standards, in varying price ranges. But remember, this is an investment in your business. No need to spend thousands of dollars on a mic but as a general rule get the highest quality mic you can afford.

> *ATR2100* This is a podcasters secret weapon. A huge mistake many business owners make when jumping into the podcasting world is forgetting about audio quality. Because podcasting is becoming a high-end platform, one that is *making* businesses, you NEED to be concerned with audio quality. But the last thing I want is for you to be so overly obsessed with how your audio sounds that you never produce an

episode. This little mic takes the stress out of creating quality sound. You can be confident that you sound good and you can now focus on delivering great content. It's a USB/XLR mic, meaning you can plug it directly into your computer (or phone, see below) and when you are ready to step up to the next level, it can transition with you.

Heil PR-40 If you are looking to get the absolute best sound for your podcast this is the mic you want. The ATR2100 will get you the best sound for the price but the Heil is the clear winner in the audio department; although it's significantly more of an investment it won't completely break the bank, and I believe it is worth it. I've been very happy with my Heil PR-40 and frequently get comments from guests about the quality of the sound I have.

There are many other microphone options to choose from, and yes, you can find them for $25, but another word of caution. As a general rule, you get what you pay for. The more you are able to spend on the mic the higher quality it will be. You are creating an AUDIO podcast. If you are going to invest in any part of this, invest in the sound of your voice. While amazing-sounding audio will not get you subscribers, bad audio will certainly cause you to lose subscribers.

RECORDERS

Once you decide on your microphone, it's time to decide on how you are going to capture your audio. You have a few options at this point. You can record directly into your computer or into a digital audio recorder. (In the Mobile Podcasting section we will cover a third option.)

Recording directly into your computer is usually where most podcasters start. That's how I did. I opened Garageband, plugged my ATR2100 in, and started talking. It works great and is a nice way to start, but maybe not where you want to stay long term.

PowerOfPodcastingBook.com

Going that route means recording into your editing software. This can save a little time since you will not have to import any of the files and you can even edit on the fly. However, there are a couple downfalls. Depending on your computer, or if you are running multiple applications, it's possible that your computer could lag or freeze at points. This can mean disruptions in your audio, or, worst-case scenario, it could crash and lose all of your recorded content. That sucks, and believe me, I know this personally. That's why I recommend eventually working your way toward recording on a digital audio recorder.

I bought my first recorder as a freshman in college to record the lectures to study from later. I think I only ever relistened to one lecture, but that little recorder got me interested in the world of podcasting. I began to use it to record my speaking events, to learn from and find ways to improve my keynotes. Eventually I started sending those recordings to the event planners that booked me.

The quality of that first recorder was not very good, but it began to open the word of podcasting to me. Nowadays, there is only one recorder I recommend and that is the Roland R-05.

This recorder can be used as an in-the-field recorder with built-in microphones, and when properly situated it does a good job of setting a scene but still gives you high-quality vocals. A microphone (like the ATR2100) can also be plugged directly into it with a one-eighth-inch XLR adapter. Or, the way I use it most often, is as a line-in recorder for the output of my mixer. For this you will need a mixer (we will cover those in the next section).

One additional note on recording audio: make it a practice of recording your audio in the highest-quality setting possible, and that usually means you should be recording in WAV instead of MP3. Your finished file will be sent out into the world as an MP3 since it's a smaller file size and more universally accepted, but we want to maintain as much of the original audio quality until the very end of the process.

MIXERS

Many first-time podcasters look to get a USB mic, mainly because they are a little intimidated by all the fancy nobs of a mixer. While a mixer is not required to produce a good show, I think it is a great addition to your studio and will allow you to have a higher-quality sound. Most of the higher-quality mics (like the Heil) only use XLR cables and while you can get a USB adapter nowadays, you still get the best sound by using an XLR cable.

So, what exactly is a mixer anyway? A mixer "mixes" various sound inputs down into one sound output. For example, it's the device that allows you to have one in-studio host, a Skype interviewee, sound clips playing from your iPad, and a second in-studio guest host all recorded on your Roland R-05 digital audio recorder. Actually, the above scenario is how my studio is set up, and a mixer makes that possible.

I am going to give you two mixer recommendations, a basic and a premium. The Mackie 802 is the clear winner, especially if you plan to do interviews or expand your studio to multiple mics or inputs one day. There are several versions of Mackie mixers, with one of the main differences being the number of channels. The amount of channels that you need will depend on the type of shows you are planning to do. I recommend eight channels. Here's why: your mic (Channel 1), Skype interviewee (Channel 2), sound clips from iPad (Channel 3), second in-studio mic (Channel 4). If you look at mixers you will notice that while they say 8 Channels, a couple of the channels are controlled by the same dials. Personally I want these four devices to be separate from each other on their own dedicated channel.

My other mixer is for those who are more price conscious. I have used this mixer for a while and still keep it around as a back-up. At about $50, the Behringer 802 is one of the best deals you will find on mixers. It is very similar to the Mackie, but the Mackie is constructed better and has a few additional features that, if you can afford it, make it a great upgrade. However, I ran my entire podcast business off the Behringer 802 for the first nine months using the same four-input set-up as described above with zero issues.

INTERVIEW RECORDING SOFTWARE

A staple of many podcasts is interviews. Depending on your set-up, you have a couple options for recording those calls. With the set-up described above in the mixer section you can simply record the conversation over Skype, Google Hangouts, FaceTime, or another service through your digital audio recorder.

This is my preferred method, since having software on your computer recording the call can slow it down and cause connection issues. Internet connections can be shaky enough as it is, so I will do anything to improve my chances of having a high-quality call.

A second option is Google Hangouts. I started off using this mainly because I wanted to record a video for the podcast to release on YouTube. I stopped this practice partly because of connection issues, but also because I don't think twenty to forty minutes of two talking heads make for very interesting video content. Video will likely make a return to some of my client's podcasts, but not in this back-and-forth Google Hangout style.

The third and most popular option is to record your Skype interview. Almost everyone these days has a familiarity with Skype, making it an easy place to connect for an interview, and eCamm's Call Recorder for Skype makes it easy to record Skype calls. It's inexpensive, highly reliable (at least as far as your Skype audio can be reliable), and simple to use. eCamm even makes a Call Record for FaceTime for all of you Mac lovers out there. If you are a PC user, sorry, but Call Recorder for Skype is only for Macs, instead try looking at Pamela. I have never had the chance to use it, but have heard many good things about it from my PC podcaster friends.

MOBILE PODCASTING

Are you a busy business person constantly traveling and on the go? Or are you looking to create a lifestyle where you are out seeing the world? Don't worry, you now have some excellent options for mobile podcasting.

From just an iPhone you could run your whole podcast without losing much, if any, audio quality. In this section of the book I'll run through a couple options to podcast on the go. Some require very little gear while others will have special equipment that's needed. I suggest that if being mobile is important to you, you test out a few of these. For some, the editing process on a iPhone might take more time than it would on a computer, but if they had to lug around their computers and set up mics each time they would never record. Find the balance between efficiency and mobility. Test a few of the options until you find the right fit and create your own workflow that makes sense for you.

First option: the laptop and mic. I won't go into too much detail with this since it's extremely similar to our main set-up. The only difference is that you might ignore the mixer and opt for a USB-only mic. If that is the case go with the ATR2100 if you have a mixer set up back at home. Another great USB mic option is the ATR2500. I know many people who actually prefer the way they sound on the ATR2500 versus the ATR2100. The 2500 is a USB-only mic, so there's no option to add a mixer, and it is a condenser mic, which means it will pick up more of the environment.

Second option is a Roland R-05. If you have a laptop back at a home-base location but would like to record a podcast while out and about, this is a great option. The Roland has an excellent built-in microphone, and you can buy a windscreen for it to help cut down on excess environmental noise.

The next option is to use your smartphone. I am an Apple fanatic (in case you haven't figured that out yet) so I will only be discussing iPhone or iPad options, the same applications or similar are likely on other devices, but you will need to do your own searching for those.

First, what's the best microphone? The built-in microphone is a good option and if you only have that, don't let it stop you from recording. Few listeners will be turned off by the sound quality produced from the built-in mic or the mic in the Apple earbuds. Other great mic options are your ATR2100 or ATR2500. To use them you will need to buy a camera connection adapter kit that contains an adapter for USB to Lighting. You can then plug in and record from a USB microphone.

A third great microphone option, and my top recommendation for a lavalier microphone, is the SmartLav from Rode. This mic is specifically designed for the iPhone. Rode also has a great app that goes along with the microphone that provides you with great setting controls. I use this set up for recording speeches and keynotes when creating online courses for clients.

Looking to add intro/outro music or play sound clips during your podcast? Check out the BossJock app. This is an iPhone and iPad app that creates a soundboard for you. Not only is this the perfect tool for doing live-to-tape podcasting on the go, but I also use this app on my iPad whenever I need to play sound clip in my studio at home. Connect the iPad to your mixer and it works perfectly.

If you need to do some editing when you are out and about, your best option currently is the Garageband app. I don't have a ton of experience with this app. It will get the job done in a pinch but I am not a huge fan. I'm still searching for a better solution for editing while mobile. For right now, I focus on recording live to tape and only use Garageband if an edit is absolutely necessary.

Once you reach that point, it is simply a matter of writing your show notes. I use Draft or Evernote to create those on the go, and post those using

Wordpress's iPhone app. The uploading and posting of a podcast from mobile devices is currently the most frustrating part. Hopefully some savvy developers soon will make this much easier (hint hint, wink wink).

PowerOfPodcastingBook.com

A PLACE TO CALL HOME

In order to create a podcast you need to have a platform: you need a place your audience can gather. Your podcast needs a home. My recommendation is that this place be a self-hosted Wordpress website.

If you have never set up a website before it can be a little intimidating, but don't worry, it's easier than you think. In this post I'll walk you through the basics step by step. By the end of the post you will have your own website up and running in less time than it takes to watch a "Game of Thrones" episode.

This website is more than just a place to send

people from your podcast. This will be the hub for your business. There are many nuances to website design that are beyond the scope of this book. However, if you would like some basic help with this process go to *YourPodcastGuru.com/website*.

Your website says a lot about your brand. You want a website that looks good, but you also want one that's powerful and easy to operate (especially if you are managing it yourself). The way to get the best of all worlds is by using a premium Wordpress theme.

Why a Premium Theme?

A theme is what gives your website character. It provides the overall feel and flow of your site. Generally, they can be very customizable by changing colors, graphics, placement and type of widgets. The theme also controls a lot of the behind-the-scenes power of your Wordpress site. They each have unique features and operate with different focuses.

When choosing a theme you will want to make sure it fits with your style, website needs, and overall business model. Too often I see platform builders who focus only on the first or second piece and completely forget about your business model needs. The website is first and foremost a business tool, it is DESIGNED to get you clients! Don't neglect this and go for a fancy-looking website where the function and conversion to clients are afterthoughts. You will regret it.

A completely custom-designed website is a waste of time and money when you starting out (eventually it might be the best option but NOT right away). A premium theme will be beautifully designed, fairly customizable, and have great technical support. You could search for Wordpress themes and get thousands of free themes. However, I think that is a bad route to take. You are running a business and your website is one of your most important tools. You want to make sure your theme is fully supported and receives updates on a regular basis. You want to minimize your risk of getting hacked. That is why you should spend the money to get a premium theme.

What to Look for in a Theme

- **Flow and Feel**. One of the first things to consider is the overall feel and flow of the theme. Try to find several examples of website that are currently running that theme. See what the owners have done with that site. What do you like about it? What do you not like about it? How well does it navigate and move prospective clients along? Go ahead and write all this down. Take screenshots and save them for when you are working on your design. This has been a huge help for me. I have an Evernote notebook dedicated to website design components I like.

- **Mobile Responsive**. In today's world, as a business owner, consultant, or speaker, one of the main goals of your site is to help you easily reach as many people as possible. Your audience is likely on the go when they are consuming your content so you want a site that looks good on any device without a lot of extra work on your part. That's why I only look for responsive themes. Many of the big premium theme sites have a search function to filter down to only responsive themes (and all my recommendations below are responsive). Another quick, secret way to tell if a theme is responsive is to grab the corner of your browser and shrink the size down. If the page changes and formats in an aesthetically pleasing, easy-to-read way then it is responsive.

- **Email Capture**. The most valuable asset your online business has is your email list. This allows you to reach out, create a strong relationship, and sell your products to your audience. Whether it's through a plugin or a built-in form, you NEED to make sure your theme has the ability to capture emails. The main function of all of my websites *is not to sell my products or services;* the main function is to get people on my email list.

My Premium WordPress Theme

Recommendations

I have three theme recommendations for you. In my eyes, these themes stand above the rest. I will walk you through each one and why I like them.

- *Divi Theme from Elegant Themes:* Elegant Themes has some of the most beautiful Wordpress themes on the web. They are a premium theme development company, so all they do is produce outstanding themes. I am a huge fan of the Divi theme. It has an outstanding drag and drop page designer which allows you to customize to your hearts content. My website is running off of the Divi Theme.

- *Get Noticed! Theme for WordPress:* I really like this theme from Michael Hyatt and Andrew Buckman. I started using this theme when it was in the very first beta format ; I liked it then and they continue to make it better and better. If you are a speaker or want to build a serious platform around blogging, you need to look into the Get Noticed! theme. The reason I choose to use this one is because of the behind-the-scenes functionality. I love the mini posts it allows you to create. That in and of itself was worth it for my speaking website, http://nickpalkowski.com.

- *New Rainmaker Platform:* This last recommendation is a little unique. Unique in that I have not used this on a live site yet. New Rainmaker is a new platform from the Copy Blogger team. It's designed with business in mind. It integrates online marketing and sales together in an easy-to-use platform. Soon I will be jumping into Rainmaker for some client sites because *everything* is under one roof, which I love.

There you have it, my three top theme recommendations for your podcasting platform site.

For the most up-to-date list visit YourPodcastGuru.com/theme.

Now it's up to you. A word of caution though: I've seen so many people get hung up on choosing the correct theme and making sure their site looks perfect before they launch. *Don't let that be you!*

The best thing you can do to grow your audience and online platform is to get your site up and start delivering value. Iterate along the way. You will likely never be satisfied with the way your site looks. That's OK. Make changes as you go. I make tweaks to mine on a weekly basis. The key is to start serving.

MEDIA HOSTING

After a website the next major topic to cover is media hosting. A media host is going to be where your audio file is stored for your podcast.

Most people will subscribe to your podcast from a directory like iTunes. iTunes gets all of your podcast information from your RSS feed. Your RSS feed is created when you publish a blog post (for podcasts we usually call these show notes but realize that show notes are blog posts). That blog post contains an audio file that your RSS feed recognizes and sends to the directories, which notifies your subscribers. Make sense so far?

Where the media host comes in is by actually placing that audio file within your blog post. Wordpress and your self-hosted servers aren't designed to support the demands of a podcast audio file, especially if it becomes popular. Basically, they use too much of the host's resources. This means they will either shut your site down or charge you a butt load of extra fees. You don't want that, especially since there is a very easy solution — a media host.

Libsyn is the main media host I recommend in this book, one other option I like is Soundcloud, but it is slightly more technical to get working. Libsyn is a media host that is set up to handle the demands of your audio files. They charge a monthly fee, depending on how much content you upload, and allow an unlimited amount of downloads. That means even if your podcast jumps from 10 listeners to 100,000 in a month you will not have to pay a penny more. I love that and use them.

DIRECTORIES

How do people find new podcasts? That is what podcast directories are for. There are several podcast directories but by far the most popular is iTunes.

This is something many new podcasters get confused about. They think that their podcast is run through iTunes; that's simply not true. iTunes is a directory. It just points people to podcasts. Kind of like a phone book. The podcast is run through your website, RSS feed, and media host.

Another major directory you will want to make sure your podcast is in is Stitcher. Submitting your podcast to a directory is pretty straightforward. For iTunes you only need to enter your podcast feed. For others you might need to add a few more details, like your show title. Once you submit to directories there is a brief approval period, but once you are approved you never need to worry about your newest episode showing up.

RECORDING PROCESS

The most important part of a podcast is, of course, your audio file. Let's run through the process of how you record that audio.

Your process might be slightly different depending on your equipment. The example process I'll use is based off of the following recommended equipment:

- ATR2100

- Computer

- Adobe Audition

Finding a quiet space is going to be very important. You will also want to think about the room set-up. A plain, empty space actually will produce bad audio quality; your sound will bounce off the surfaces and reverberate back into the recording. Adding furniture, carpet, or even acoustic panels will help absorb the sound.

If you are on the road or looking for a cheap solution you can record in a closet full of clothes or throw a comforter over top of you while recording (yes, I am dead serious).

The ATR2100 is a USB mic so all you have to do is plug it into the computer, open your recording software (Adobe Audition is my recommendation), and start delivering your amazing content!

Recording for Interviews

If your podcast has interviews, the recording process is going to be slightly different. Ideally, you and your guest have quality microphones like the ATR2100. I'd even consider sending one as a gift just to make sure it's quality audio.

I generally recommend using Skype to conduct the interview (or Zoom.us but not many people are familiar with that service and I want to make the process as pain-free for guests as possible).

You will want to connect you mic, open Skype after installing Call Recorder (YourPodcastGuru.com/CallRecorder) and then call your guest. At FreeGiftFromNick.com I've included a checklist that you can use and send to your guests to make sure everything is set up correctly for the best sounding audio.

EDITING PROCESS

Once you have your raw recording it's time to begin editing. I recommend using the Adobe Audition software to edit. At $20 per month with a Creative Cloud subscription it is worth the investment for high-quality sound.

After importing the audio, I add the intro and outro as well as any stock segment bumpers or commercials. Once all of those are in the correct spot, I do a quick check of the audio levels. For most episodes, I am done at that point and I simply export in MP3 format. However, occasionally I'll need to edit Skype issues or will want to remove sections where we had to pause in the recording process. For the most part, if I was part of the recording process I can do this very quickly because I always capture the relative time code of any issues. If it is a client's recording I often will need to listen to the complete recording, pausing to edit any issues I notice.

SET-UP AND SUBMIT

The Power of Podcasting

This is one of the parts of podcasting that many would-be podcasters freak out over, for no real reason. The setting up and submitting of your podcast feeds to directories can be a little technical, but it is VERY well documented all over the internet. Now, in this book I'll give you the highlighted steps to the set up process I recommend. At FreeGiftFromNick.com there is a click-by-click video walk-through of the entire process so you just need to follow along and your podcast will be iTunes-ready in no time.

First you need to make sure you have all the pieces required including:

- Fully edited first episode
- Cover art (1400 by1400 pixels or 2800 by 2800 pixels)
- Podcast title
- Author name
- Podcast description
- Shownotes for your first episode

- Podcast tagline

Then download the two plug-ins for your Wordpress website that will make your life significantly easier: Blubrry Powerpress and Pretty Links.

Once those two plug-ins are installed, you need to publish your first podcast episode. In order to generate a RSS feed required for submitting your podcast, you need to have one episode that is live on your site.

First, go over to your media host (Libsyn) and upload your audio along with the episode title and shownotes. Once published there will be a "Direct Download URL", copy that. Paste the Direct Download URL in the "Podcast Episode" box that can be found under the content section of a new post on your website.

After pasting that URL go through and fill in the shownotes, episode title, and image for that episode. Be sure to also format it in the way you would like. I also recommend adding a "Podcast" category to the post. I've found this useful for lumping together all the podcasts.

Once your first podcast episode is published, go into the settings of the Powerpress plug-in. I recommend switching to advanced setup and filling in all the information in the appropriate spots. (Again, in the video found at FreeGiftFromNick.com I'll walk you through each of the settings and checkboxes so you know what exact set-up is right for you.)

At this point, Powerpress will take care of creating your podcast RSS feed, and tell you what feed should be submitted to iTunes. Copy that feed URL.

The next step is to go to the podcast section of the iTunes store. There you will see a link to "Submit a Podcast." If you are not already signed in, iTunes will ask for your Apple ID. You must have an iTunes account in order to submit a podcast. Once signed in, you will be taken to a page asking for your Podcast Feed URL. Paste the feed from Powerpress. iTunes will then gather all the information found on that feed and display the title, artwork, description, etc. Review and then press submit, and you have successfully submitted a podcast to iTunes!

Your podcast will not immediately appear. Apple will review your show to make sure it meets all the requirements. This can occasionally take up to a week but I've been getting a less than 24-hour turn around with my last few shows.

The process for submitting to other directories is similar. I will have a complete list of recommended directories in the Appendix and will keep an updated list with the resources found at FreeGiftFromNick.com.

Once you have submitted your show to the directories, the rest of the podcast publishing process is easy. Each time you want to publish a new episode, simply create a new post. The RSS feed will automatically send it out to the directories.

HOW TO DIFFERENTIATE YOURSELF

What makes you unique? How are you going to stand out?

Those are the questions you need to ask when starting your podcast. It's not about finding a niche that has never been done before, in fact that is usually a bad move, it's more about finding your own voice; finding an approach that is uniquely you.

Before you ever hit the record button for the first time, you need to get to work.

Do your Recon Work

This is the first assignment I give all my clients. Find the top three to five podcasts in your niche, and listen to several of their episodes while taking notes. What do you like about their show? What do you not like about it, what turns you off? What is their listener's biggest challenge?

Now, how can you do it better? Brainstorm ways you can make your show more appealing. Think about how you can solve the biggest challenge that listeners have. It's those things that will set you apart. Not your fancy intro music but being able to solve your audience's needs, **that** is going to be why people to listen.

Next, make sure you have a few podcasts you like to listen to in different markets. Look at the way they approach podcasting about their topics. What are some unique things they do that you can incorporate into your show? To truly differentiate yourself from others in your industry you need to look for ideas outside your industry; that's from where the best innovations come. A great example of this is the drive-thru window. Most people think of fast food, but that wasn't always the case. One day a restaurant owner was using the drive-up window at a bank when he got the idea to try a drive-thru window at his restaurant, the world hasn't been the same since.

The one caution I want to give: don't look for uniqueness just for the sake of being unique. Your differentiation should ALWAYS be in service to your audience. It should give them a better experience in some way. It's not about you standing out. It's about providing more value.

No Rules

The best thing about podcasting is that there are no rules. Your podcast can be designed in any way you like. It could be 1 minute or 4 hours long (yes, there are podcasts in both of those extremes). It could be highly produced National Public Radio-style show or you could get on a conference phone line. You can include tips, interviews, case studies, or read blog posts. It's up to you. That's why the best thing about podcasting is that there are no rules!

The worst thing about podcasting is … there are no rules!

This can often leave people paralyzed, unsure of what direction to take or how to proceed. Or those who do often fall into the trap of doing exactly what everyone else is doing, instead of taking advantage of their ability to make it their own flavor.

BRANDING

An important element that often gets overlooked by many eager podcasters is their podcast branding. Remember, the purpose of podcasting is to grow your business. To do that your podcast needs to 1) tie into an overall business strategy and 2) help people understand what to expect from you.

Creating a clever name or some abstract, flashy cover art for your show is often the wrong approach. The question you should be asking is "Does this make it easy for a listener to understand what I'm about?" Keep this question in mind as you go through each aspect of branding, because your brand is much more than what color your logo is, your brand tells your story. It's how you communicate. It's your reputation and your values. You are your brand.

Now, let's walk through each of the major brand assets you will need when creating a podcast.

TITLE

The title of your podcast is the most prominent and important branding asset. A well designed title performs several key functions. It's because of the title's importance that many people can be tripped up and spend far too long procrastinating on choosing a title.

A title should be intriguing to your ideal audience. When searching in iTunes are people drawn to click on your show to hear more? Your title should communicate what the show is about and who the audience is.

A well-designed title also helps your podcast be discovered by your ideal audience when they are searching for keywords in iTunes. That means if your ideal audience is likely to type in "goal setting" into the search bar, and your podcast has "goals" or "goal setting" in your title, you are golden.

Don't worry about being super clever. In fact, titles that are too clever can actually hurt your listenership. If people don't get the reference or understand what your podcast is about, you will lose listeners. As a rule, stick to a straightforward name that explains what the podcast is about or who your audience is. Remember, the goal of your title, cover art, and description is to get people to click and listen to one episode. Once that happens, then you can start being clever and really letting your personality shine.

COVER ART

The cover art is going to be the first thing people see about your podcast. You want to make sure it catches their attention. I recommend keeping the cover art simple and uncluttered. The artwork also needs to be visible on a small screen (iPhone) but iTunes requires a higher resolution photo. It should be between 1400 by 1400 pixels and 2800 by 2800 pixels. I recommend going with the highest resolution iTunes will allow. That helps future-proof your podcast and ensure that it looks great even on a TV.

Should you do your own cover art? Many new podcasters do, and if you are starting out without any audience at all I think that is OK. I would recommend at least using a resource like Canva.com. They have a Podcast Cover Art template that helps make sure you don't make a mess of your artwork. However, if you have even a moderate audience already built through another channel like a blog or email list, you should get your cover professionally designed. The old saying, "Don't judge a book by its cover" simply isn't true. We judge books, and podcasts, by the way they look. Make sure yours will stand out in the sea of podcasts in iTunes.

SHOW DESCRIPTION

If someone makes it to your description you already attracted their eye with your cover design, and got them interested with your title. Now is the time to tell them what to expect from the podcast. With the description you should give them an idea of who this podcast is for and what they can expect to get from listening.

A well-written description will not only communicate that basic information to the listener but also will intrigue, motivate, and entice them to take action. In addition, I recommend you tell them what to expect. Is this a weekly show? What day will the podcast be released? Are you doing interviews or sharing case studies? All of that can be explained in a succinct description.

iTunes allows for up to 4,000 characters in a description; I don't recommend using all of them. Remember that most people will subscribe to your podcast from their mobile phones. Keep your description relatively short so they don't need to scroll much to read the whole description.

AUTHOR NAME

Your author name — sounds simple enough right? Well, you should put a little more thought into it than simply typing out your first and last name. This also is searchable. Now, I don't recommend keyword stuffing it with a bunch of random famous names so your podcast shows up whenever someone searches that name (yes, that is a real, far too common practice).

However, you can add a few keywords that are relevant to you and your podcast. For example, Your Name: Keynote Speaker, Success Coach, and Lifestyle Entrepreneur. This is great if your podcast is focused around lifestyle and personal development. Don't get too creative. Remember you want these to be words people might actually search for. Trust me no one is searching for "Biz Expert", "Writerpreneur", or any other "-preneur" for that matter.

TAGLINE

The tagline, it seems like a great way to get across in a short sentence what your podcast is all about. However, at the time of this writing, while iTunes still asks for your tagline, it doesn't actually appear anywhere in iTunes.

Does this mean you can skip it? No. While a person looking for a new podcast to subscribe to might not see your tagline, that doesn't mean it's not factored in when showing search results. That's a chance you don't want to take, so spend some time and think of a keyword-based tagline.

Besides, a well-crafted tagline can be used over and over again to quickly explain what your podcast is about. From the intro bumper to social media, to emails to that random run-in with the cute girl in the coffee shop who asks "What do you do?", the tagline has many uses. It also will help keep you focused in the right direction when it comes to content creation.

INTRO/OUTRO

Two of your biggest, most valuable branding elements are your intro and outro. These helps set the tone for your episodes. Many listeners might never read your descriptions, visit your website, or even see your cover art after they subscribe to your show, but each time they listen to an episode, they will hear your intro and outro.

A great intro has a theme song that helps set the mood for the episode. Some are inspirational, some will pump you up, others will get you relaxed. This is all part of your branding so make sure to find a theme song that aligns with what you want to communicate. Most podcasters will want to have a stock intro created with their theme song and a short voiceover that explains what the podcast is all about. For help creating your intros go to YourPodcastGuru.com/BookResources for a list of resources, from where to find royalty-free songs to complete audio-branding services.

Your outro is another important element of your podcast. In my opinion it is an element that does not receive enough attention from most podcasters. This is the last thing your listeners will hear, so make use of it. Use your outro to reinforce the tone you set with your podcast, such as by replaying the intro theme song, but also use it to summarize the episode or give your listeners important call-to-actions (CTAs) like subscribing or leaving reviews. One warning about your outros: don't overwhelm your listener with too many CTAs; you might want to try just one. Here is a list of important CTAs you can rotate through in different episodes: Subscribing in iTunes, leaving a review, sharing your podcast with someone else, tweeting about your podcast, signing up for your email list, or leaving a question for you.

An important thing to remember is that most of your listeners are listening on their mobile devices. They might be driving, they might be working out, or doing the dishes. When giving a CTA make it as easy as possible to follow that action. For example, if you want them to subscribe to the podcast create a link to your podcast that uses YourPodcastName.com/iTunes to redirect them. This is easy to do using a Wordpress plugin called Pretty Links.

I've recently started directing people to send a text message to opt-in to an email list instead of asking them to go to a website to sign up for emails. The reason I love this option is because it's so quick and easy for most people. You will need a compelling reason for why people should opt-in; they are not going to "sign up for updates." Their cell number is too personal for that. But if you have a valuable opt-in, you will get more subscribers than an email offer ever would.

EPISODE ARTWORK

Earlier we covered the important branding aspect of your cover art for your podcast but now I want to talk about a branding resource many podcasters put little or no thought to. Your episode artwork. This is an image that goes along with an episode. No, episode art is not required (unlike your cover art), but it can bring that extra value and shareablilty to your episode.

In a world dominated by social media, especially picture-based social media, creating a unique image for each episode will drastically increase the engagement and ultimately listens for your podcast. I recommend finding an engaging picture that relates to the topic of your episode, and creating a text overlay using Photoshop, Keynote, or Canva. The text can be the title of the episode or an important quotation. At the time of this writing, I usually place the cover art of the podcast and the episode URL on the image as well. This helps make sure that when your image is shared, people are able to find your podcast.

SHOW FLOW

What should your show look like? How should it be structured? I want to reiterate that one of the best things about podcasting is that *there are no rules.* If you don't find this helpful and would prefer to have some guard rails, here is my recommendation for the flow of a show:

- Episode number
- Introduction
- In this episode/hook
- Main content
- Special segment or commercial
- Closing and call-to-action

Episode number: This is where you announce what episode you are presenting. It's nice to have this to give the listener some context. I know some podcasters who will give the name of the episode or do a teaser on the content that will be covered in the episode.

Introduction: This is the official kick-off to the show. If you are a regular podcast listener (which you should be!) you have likely heard them. There is usually a theme song and either the show host or a special voiceover announcer gives the title and tagline of the show. Doing your own intro is a good way to start, especially if you have a limited budget. To get a list of my recommended resources for introductions visit YourPodcastGuru.com/BookResources.

In This Episode/Hook: This is where you want to give the listener a very direct statement about what you will be covering in the episode, **such as** "Six tips for managing email overwhelm" or some sort of teaser hook. The former approach is designed to allow listeners to choose if this episode is worth their time, the latter is designed to entice them to keep listening in order to find the answer.

Main Content: The meat and potatoes. This is where you deliver the goods, provide the value, bring home the bacon. (This is why I shouldn't write before breakfast). This segment should be the bulk of your show.

Special segment or commercial: You might choose to have a special segment, like a tip of the week, or bring in a guest to talk about a topic. This is also where I would recommend you put in your "commercial." For some podcasters, this might be a sponsorship ad, but for most this should be a quick promotion for one of your products or services.

Closing and call-to-action: It's time to bring the show home. Give a quick wrap-up. I like to include some sort of take-action challenge that gets people thinking about how to start implementing the content you covered. You should also give some more standard CTAs including leaving a review, subscribing to podcast, sharing podcast, subscribing to your email list, or buying your product. These all don't need to happen every time but get into the habit of regularly mentioning them.

RELEASING THE SHOW

The way to make your podcast the most effective is to build in habit for your audience by releasing your content on a consistent basis. Whatever release schedule you choose make sure it is a frequency with which you can stick. Being too ambitious and then not keeping a regular release schedule will hurt you more than throttling back at the beginning to a schedule you can maintain for the long term. Many soon-to-be podcasters are concerned about the New & Noteworthy section of iTunes (we will cover this more later), wanting to release shows every day to take advantage of this. Bad idea. Your business is about much more than the eight-week New & Noteworthy period. Yes, I think the New & Noteworthy section is awesome and a great opportunity, but you need to think long term. Do what is best for your business, and the relationship you are developing with your potential clients.

There are several options on release frequency: monthly, weekly, daily. My recommended option is to do a weekly release of a 20- to 30-minute episode.

A weekly episode is great because it helps create a habit with your audience. They get used to hearing from you week after week. That's your ultimate goal. Not to have the most number of downloads but to create an audience that is eagerly anticipating your new content. Weekly episodes appear to be the minimum effective dose, you will see great results without wasting time on extra work. Lately it seems that everyone wants to do a daily podcast. For a few (a select few), this is a great strategy but for most it is a lot of wasted effort. If you have never created a podcast before or don't have a large following already, or if there is not a compelling reason for your niche to have a daily show, stay away from it. You will have great results with a weekly podcasts without driving yourself mad with trying to keep pace.

PowerOfPodcastingBook.com

THE CONTENT

PowerOfPodcastingBook.com

WHAT TO TALK ABOUT…

But I'm Not An Expert … What do I talk about?

That is the No. 1 objection to doing a podcast I get most. People are unsure if they have what it takes to create a podcast. They never received their expert certificate and think they have nothing to offer.

Let me be very clear about this: You are an expert. You have content and information that will be helpful to others. That's the key.

You do not need to be an expert in the academic, traditional sense that you receive awards from the president for being top in your field. That's not the type of expert we need. Let me show you the kind of expert you need to be with this quick illustration:

Imagine you are back in kindergarten. Remember how awesome those days were?! You were encouraged to take naps in the middle of the day (a practice you should still be doing, but that's another book). Naps, Play-Doh, Legos, and recess ... it was awesome! But do you remember the frustration of trying to learn how to tie your shoes? No one wanted to be that one kid still wearing velcro shoes because they have yet to master the rabbit ears. To that frustrated, struggling kindergartner, the first-grader who laces up his own Nikes is an expert.

It's not about knowing all the answers or being able to answer every question. It's about being a few steps ahead of everyone else. It's about being able and willing to show them the way. It's about being able to speed up or ease the journey. And you, future podcaster, are that type of expert in some area already.

If you are running your own business there is no question that you already are an expert. You know the topic your business covers better than your potential clients. That is extremely valuable to the right audience. Your goal is simply to share that knowledge. It's to educate your current and potential customers with the information they need to make a smart, well-informed buying decision.

Say it with me, "I am an expert!"

Still not sure what to talk about? This next exercise will help you answer that question.

10.10s

The 10.10s exercise is one that leads to great podcast content that you (as the expert on your topic) can often overlook.

First, grab a piece of paper and a pen (seriously, set down the book and do this. I'll wait …).

Next, I want you to think about the interactions you have with clients or potential clients. What are the questions they commonly ask? Come up with a list of the ten most asked questions.

Have your list done yet? The next step you want to do is think about what your clients don't know they don't know. Create a list of questions that your clients should ask to help them make the best purchasing experience possible.

You now have a list of twenty questions. Go through and for each one write a one- to two-sentence statement that encapsulates not necessarily the answer, but why this answer matters to your potential client and their interaction with your product.

The Power of Podcasting

Congratulations. You have the basis for twenty future podcasts. Your job will be to elaborate on the question, why it matters, and what steps your audience needs to take to remedy their problem.

Will each of these be a separate episode? Not necessarily, but they could be. Feel free to experiment with episode length or combine a couple of questions. Once you start posting these episodes be on the lookout for other questions your clients or prospective clients have. Don't be afraid to directly ask your audience what topics or questions they would like to hear discussed.

A mentor of mine, Pat Flynn of the Smart Passive Income podcast, launched a separate podcast to answering his audience's questions (The Ask Pat podcast. I highly recommend subscribing to it). In order to help ensure he had people submitting questions he offered a free T-shirt to anyone whose question he used on the air. That's a great avenue to consider especially if you already have an online following.

TOPIC LISTS

An alternative to the 10.10s exercise is to create a running subtopic list. Every major topic area has at least a couple subtopics within it. Create a list of these that you find interesting or think your audience needs to know.

Keep a running list of these. I keep mine in Evernote on my phone and whenever a new topic idea comes up, I just add it to the list. I am slowly working my way through the list at random, picking out the subtopic I am most interested in talking about on any particular day then doing a show about it. Once I do a show I move the idea to another list of completed show topics with the episode number in which I talked about it so if I ever decided to do an advanced episode on that topic or re-do the episode, I know where I can find it.

Some of the best, most listened-to episodes are how-to episodes. These are ones that walk your audience through a process in a very step-by-step way. This how to topic can be done in a single episode or, depending on the topic, it can be a how-to series where each step in the process gets its very own podcast episode.

I always think it's good to experiment with different episode structures and content areas, but be sure to listen to your audience. Your current audience will help you decide what direction to go with the show. Make note of episode downloads — is a certain type of structure regularly getting more listens? Pay attention to the unsolicited feedback you get — are you hearing about how awesome a certain type of episode is? Lastly, don't be afraid to ask your audience. Do a call-out in an episode for feedback, or create a listener survey. The information you get will be extremely valuable.

CASE STUDIES

Another great topic idea is case studies.

Feature people who either use your product or exemplify what you teach. These don't need to be famous people or highly successful by any means. They can be people who are just starting their journey, but the case studies you use should be able to guide the listeners or get them thinking about the way they are doing things in their lives.

One podcaster who I think does a phenomenal job of case studies is Pat Flynn on his Smart Passive Income podcast. He brings on regular people, people you never would have known otherwise, and shares their success stories, journey, and lessons in creating passive income. In fact, these case studies are often more popular than his interview with the big names like Gary Vaynerchuk. This is because most people can't relate to the level of the Gary Vees of the world, but they can relate to the story of the couple down the street that is making six figures a month by following the principles Pat teaches. That seems attainable. Their path seems like one anyone can follow.

INTERVIEWS

Perhaps the most popular way to create podcast content right now is interviews. It seems like every new podcast out there is doing some sort of interview show. Now, that's for a good reason. Interview shows have a lot of benefits. However, don't settle on doing an interview show just yet.

First, let's look at the benefits of an interview show. A major one, if you are at all nervous about sitting in front of a microphone, is that they are an easy way to produce content. You are able to sit down ahead of time to write out questions and can let your interviewee take it from there. Another big benefit is that you are able to leverage that person's audience to expand your listener base, since many in their audience will want to hear the interview they did with you. Both very legitimate and good reasons for an interview show.

Now, here is the downfall of the interview

show. For one, you still need to be a good interviewer. A set of scripted questions will only get you so far because they depend on the quality of guest you have to really get your show to that next level. A good interviewer is able to go down different paths, and knows when to deviate from the script to pursue a more fruitful route. Second, and for me, most important, when you are conducting an interview the person you are bringing on is seen as the expert. From a journalistic standpoint there is nothing wrong with that, but our focus for creating a podcast is to help you develop your business. That doesn't happen if you are not seen as an expert. You might gain an audience of people who want to listen to your interviews but then you are trying to turn your podcast into a business, which is another, much more difficult, path.

So, to interview or not interview? My answer is yes, you should do both. I suggest you do a combination of interviews and solo episodes to get the best of both worlds. When you interview people, it brings a fresh angle to your content, which is a good thing. It allows your audience to learn about areas in which you are not an expert, and it helps expose you to a new audience. By mixing those interviews with solo shows, you are able to dive into topics you about which you have passion and expertise. It allows you to share your story and builds your credibility, which will ultimately grow your business. The exact mix is up to you, but I would suggest you have at least one of each every month.

YOUR FIRST EPISODE

One of the nicest aspects of podcasting is that your listeners can easily go back into the archives to listen to old shows. This means a new listener could find your podcast at Episode 32 and then immediately go back through and binge-listen to every previous episode. You would be surprised at how often that happens.

That's why I recommend my clients record a specific type of first episode. Many of your new listeners will find your latest episode but then, wanting to learn more about you and your background after they listen to that latest episode, will immediately jump back to Episode 1.

To provide the greatest value to your listeners, your first episode should focus on you and the podcast. It should be a brief overview of your background and the major life events that have lead you to your current business and direction, plus an overview of what to expect in future episodes of the podcast. You can dive into your first piece of major content if you want, but it's not necessary. Don't worry too much about the length of this episode either; over or under time doesn't matter much, but if it's drastically different, be sure to mention what will be your standard podcast episode length going forward.

It's all about setting up expectations.

STRUCTURING YOUR SHOW

One of the best things about podcasting is that there are no rules. You can set up your show in any way that you like, from interviews, to one-minute tips, to four-hour episodes. You control the topics you cover. You control how often you release a new episode.

The bad thing about podcasts is there are no rules.

That can sometimes feel paralyzing because there are so many options and decisions to make. We can have the urge to wait until we have it figured out perfectly. In this section I want to help ease your angst by giving you a few recommendations that have worked well with my clients. But before we dive in I want to emphasize that this is not the only way to go. Feel free to experiment and to be unique. In fact, if your niche is already filled with podcasts a unique approach might yield the best results.

EPISODE FLOW

What should your show look like? How should it be structured? I want to reiterate that one of the best things about podcasting is that ***there are no rule*** but if you don't find this helpful and would prefer to have some guard rails, here is my recommendation for the flow of a show.

- Episode number
- Introduction
- In this episode/hook
- Main content
- Special segment or commercial
- Closing and Call-To-Action

Episode number: This is simply where you announce what episode you are on. It's nice to have this to give the listener some context on. I know some podcasters who will give the name of the episode or even do a little teaser on the content that will be covered in the episode.

Introduction: This is the official kick-off to the show. If you are a regular podcast listener (which you should be!) you have likely heard them. There is usually a theme song and either the show host or a special voice over announcer gives the title and tagline of the show. Doing your own intro is a good way to start, especially if you have a limited budget. To get a list of my recommended resources for introductions visit, YourPodcastGuru.com/BookResources.

In This Episode/Hook: This is where you want to either give the listener a very direct statement about what you will be covering in the episode, "Six Tips For Managing Email Overwhelm" or some sort of teaser hook. The former approach is designed to allow them to choose if this episode is worth their time, the latter is designed to entice them to keep listening in order to find the answer.

Main Content: The meat and potatoes. This is where you deliver the good, provide the value, bring home the bacon. (This is why I shouldn't write before breakfast). This segment should be the bulk of your show.

Special segment or commercial: You might choose to have a special segment like tip of the week, or bring in a recurring guest to talk about a topic. This is also where I would recommend you put in your "commercial." For some podcasters, this might be a sponsorship ad, but for most this should be a quick promotion for one of your products or services. I'll dive into these in a little more detail soon.

Closing and Call-To-Action: It's time to bring the show home. Give a quick wrap up. I like to include some sort of take action challenge that gets people at least thinking about how to start implementing the content you covered. You should also give some more standard CTAs including a) leaving a review b) subscribing to podcast c) sharing podcast d) subscribing to your email list or e) buying your product. These all don't need to happen every time but get into the habit of regularly mentioning them. In fact, if you are creating stock outros you should consider create separate ones for each of your main CTA's I have started this recently with some of my clients only giving one action step in the outro and have seen a great response so far.

Also, feel free to be a little more creative with your podcast CTA every once in a while. Ask people to take an Instagram photo of where they are listening to your show and tag you. Ask people to email the show to one specific person and copy you on the email. Think about how you could get people involved and engaged without simply doing the "subscribe to my podcast" standard CTA every single time.

MILESTONES

This is the segment I've been most excited about lately. By no means is it unique to me, but I've had my clients thinking about ways they can begin to incorporate this into there shows.

The first podcast that really made me take notice of the milestone segment is Internet Business Mastery with Jeremy and Jason. At the end of each episode they do a spot called Money Milestones in which they give a quick shout-out to a listener or coaching client who made their first dollar online. Don't miss the power of this. They take the time to praise, and congratulate a listener who is making progress. This little action helps increase engagement with podcast listeners because more people will reach out to share their

Money Milestones. It also serves as a huge inspiration piece for people who haven't started down the path to making money online because they hear the excitement that the Milestoners have and see that it is possible. How can you incorporate something similar in your podcast.

Milestones are a great way to build in listener engagement, but they are not the only way you can do this. A simple one is to read listener reviews. Grabbing your latest review on iTunes, reading it on air, and thanking not only that person but also everyone who has left a review will build one more level of engagement with your audience.

Another engagement technique is to record live shows. This can be logistically difficult, and it helps if you already have some following so people will show up to interact with you at your live shows. The technology behind it is very straightforward, and I'd recommend using Google Hangouts on Air and reading the comments people leave. A podcast that does this well is "The Self Publishing Podcast" with Johnny B. Truant,

Sean Platt, and David Wright.

Answering questions on your show is another great way to build audience engagement. It could be a segment you have at the end of the podcast, or lately there is rise in the "Ask podcasts". My favorite being "Ask Pat" with Pat Flynn, or "48 Days" with Dan Miller. These are two podcasts different, but similar approaches. Both only answer questions but "48 Days" is a 48-minute show in which Dan reads email questions and answers them. While "Ask Pat" is a short 10-minute episode in which he plays an audio question and gives his answer.

However you do it will depend on your topic, your audience, and your style, but find a way to get some audience engagement going. This will dramatically increase your number of raving, dedicated fans.

SHOWNOTES

Show notes can be a great way to enhance the quality of your podcast. Every podcast is created from an RSS feed. Most podcasters do this through a blog so it's very natural to include some type of written description about what to expect in the post. I'm a firm believer that creating a high-quality, engaging post will entice new listeners to check out the podcast.

Your show notes are also a great place to include the links to the resources mentioned in your podcast. This is helpful to your listeners because when they first listen, many will be working out, driving or otherwise unable to stop and visit a webpage you mention. If you keep your naming convention consistent, then it will be easy for your listeners to find the show notes for any episode no matter when they listen. For example, I'm a fan of a three-digit episode number as the permalink for each podcast, such as YourWebsite.com/000. This allows you to give a quick, easy-to-remember URL in the audio of your episode instead of something like, YourWebsite.com/This-Is-Ridiculous-To-Remember

"But Nick, what about the SEO?!?" Excellent question, my friend. You do get some search engine optimization benefit from having keywords in the URL. Although it is a small benefit, I still like to keep keywords there, so what I do is allow Wordpress to create the permalink as it naturally would, but then I use a plug-in called Pretty Links (a must-have plug-in in my book) to create an audio-friendly URL. I use Pretty Links for almost every resource I recommend. This helps get people used to typing in my site address, but most importantly, it allows me to send them directly to the exact resource I recommend. In the back of this book all of the links under the Resource section were created with Pretty Links. I love this plug-in.

Like I mentioned in the branding section, I believe an episode image can help make the post more engaging and more shareable. In my general flow, the image goes at the top of the show notes, followed by a couple paragraphs describing the episode, then a bullet-point list of some major takeaways (with time stamps), the podcast player, subscribe buttons, resources mentioned in the episode, and lastly, an email opt-in offer.

ENHANCED SHOWNOTES

The show notes I described above were rather elaborate and will be much better quality than most podcasters take the time to produce. However, I think you can do an even better job. Enhanced show notes go beyond what was mentioned above in a few ways, but in order for the listeners to get the enhanced show notes I would have them opt-in to an email or SMS list.

Your enhanced show notes could contain a few different things. They could simply be much more detailed with a full time stamp of the major takeaways. They could be full transcripts. My favorite is one-sheet checklist or cheat sheet — something that walks listeners through the material you're teaching.

The Power of Podcasting

THE FUNNEL

PowerOfPodcastingBook.com

THE FUNNEL PHILOSOPHY

My approach to business is simple at its core — I want to create funnels. A funnel is wide at the top and narrows as you move down the funnel. This is how I view every business, is it moving people down the funnel?

At the top of the funnel people are just being introduced to your business, they know little to nothing about you, but there is no relationship with you. As you begin to build that relationship by consistently adding value they slowly start to move down the funnel. They go from consuming free content to being paying customers to being raving fans.

As your audience moves down the funnel their relationship with you grows and their lifetime value as a customer grows. This is how you build a powerful business. It's now common knowledge that selling to a new customer is significantly harder than selling to an existing customer. That's why our ultimate focus is to increase your customer's lifetime value. Yes, we want to keep filling the new customer bucket, but we want to spend more time developing and deepening your relationship with your existing customers.

That is the main tenant of the Funnel Philosophy — increase you relationship with your audience and increase their lifetime value. You do this by developing seven levels of products. I'll go through each below but I want you to remember that this is the overall business structure. It's likely (in fact, highly encouraged) that there will be several mini funnels built within this overall structure. For example, when you launch your medium-priced product you might do so by giving away free content, using an email opt-in offer, and then asking for the sale. Start approaching everything in your business with the Funnel Philosophy and you will soon start maximizing your business.

PODCAST

The podcast is the perfect first level of the funnel. They are a very low-risk product for listeners. Your audience doesn't need to "pay" in any way, not even with an email, to hear your content.

A podcast is also the easiest-to-consume medium. It requires no screen time, can travel with them, and can be listened to while doing other activities. Plus, podcasts give your listeners a peek into who you are in a way that blog posts and other written content just can't.

EMAIL LIST

Your goal is to move people down the funnel. Your best clients are the ones who have moved down the funnel the furthest and have even brought others with them. However, it's rare that people will move through your funnel without your offering them the option to.

Two mistakes I see business owners make are: not asking people to move down their funnel and asking too much before the relationship is established. The latter is akin to asking a girl to marry you on the first date. That's the best way to ensure there won't be a second date.

The first thing you ask your listeners to do should be to subscribe to an email list. I am a huge advocate for building a strong email list. If listeners are willing to "pay you" with their email addresses you know they are more valuable clients. They are ready and willing to advance their relationships with you.

The reason the email list needs to be the first thing you ask for is because it is your most valuable asset. When set up right, an email list is potentially even more valuable to a business than your podcast. The email list is where sales are made. The podcast is how you develop the relationship and inform the client, but it's the email list that walks them through the sales process.

Also, don't fall into the trap that I see with many email lists — only sending out broadcast emails. If the only email you send out is a weekly email letting people know about the latest podcast or blog post, you are heading in the right direction — many don't even communicate with their lists at all — but you are leaving a lot on the table. You NEED to set up a good autoresponder sequence.

The purpose of your main autoresponder sequence should be to let people know who you are, what you offer, and how you can help them. It takes time to develop this first introductory autoresponder. You will need to sit down and think about what a complete beginner needs to know and the best way to walk them through the process. But it's a **do it once, use it forever** action. Once you complete that autoresponder sequence it will pay off for you over and over again.

LOW PRICE PRODUCT

Are you ready to start making some money? You are adding value to your audience on a regular basis and you have a growing email list. Now it's time to get some customers. This is the biggest, most important step in your funnel: converting an audience that is consuming content for free to paying for content. It's generally recognized that acquiring a new customers costs between 4-to-6 times more than selling to current clients.

Sticking with The Funnel Philosophy will make this transition as smooth as possible. Your next step in the funnel is to create a low-priced product. The point of this product is not to help you retire early, in fact it's very likely you won't make much money off this, even if you do well, but that's not the objective of this product. Your goal is to start creating a list of buyers. You want to know who finds your content valuable enough to pull out their wallets and make a purchase.

This is key. It sets you up for success down the

road. Think of this product like that pack of gum in the checkout aisle. Buying your product needs to be a no-brainer for people. You want to deliver great value at a price that requires very little consideration. The actual price point will depend on your industry and brand, but think – 99 cents to $20 as a good starting spot.

LOW-PRICED SUBSCRIPTION

Now that your audience is starting to move down the funnel it's time to create the next level of product for them — a low-priced subscription service.

Recurring revenue is the holy grail of entrepreneurdom. Having a predictable stream of revenue that comes in month after month without the extra work of acquiring new clients is extremely valuable in building a solid business foundation.

For this level of the funnel, look to create a

monthly subscription that is low priced. Again, this depends on your industry, but likely a $5 to $25 range is a good one. Ideally, this is a more passive form of income for you, meaning you are already creating the content or it's a slight variation of content you are already creating. For example, if you are a writer who produces books on a regular basis, you could create a subscription program in which your raving fans can get your books for free before you release them on Amazon. For interview podcasts, after you create your normal show, record a second interview right away that goes more in-depth or is more tactically focused and then make it available on a special membership page.

The objective of this level is to provide you with that stable foundation of income. Hopefully this program will be able to cover many of your expenses quickly and because it will be recurring, you can be confident that you have a certain amount of money coming in regularly. This confidence is important. It will free you up to work on projects that could move the needle significantly for you versus just trying to make sure you come up with something to pay the electric bill.

MEDIUM-PRICED PRODUCT

Now you have some loyal followers. Now you are growing a real business in a smart way. Now it's time to create some real income. Now it's time for a medium priced product.

A medium-priced product is about $100 to $997, again varying greatly by industry. This product generally includes a vast amount of how-to information. It is usually a multimedia course, perhaps a workbook with a handful of short videos. It should be a product for people who want some guidance, and is mostly a self-study product. I would also recommend that, after you create the content, it require very little involvement on your part. Ideally it can be delivered electronically while you sleep, and your client can complete it without your involvement at all.

The main function of this level is to create a

passive form of income for you. That's not to say you can "passively" (read: lazily) put this product together. "Passive" and "lazy" unfortunately seem to be linked in many people's minds. They are not one and the same. If your product is not high quality and high value to your customers, it will not sell. It does not deserve to sell. "Passive" in this case refers to your involvement in the delivery of the product.

HIGH-PRICED PRODUCT

Now it's time to bring in some real money. It's time to create a high-priced, high-value product.

For many this will be an online course, something that solves a major problem for the audience you've built. This needs to be done in a very professional, high-value way. If you are going to be charging $1,000 to $5,000 or higher, you need to be able to deliver a return on that investment of five to ten times what your clients are paying. That's no small order, so before you start creating your first high-priced product, be sure you sit down and actually evaluate if you can deliver on this promise.

This product will likely not be a passive one like the medium-priced product. It will require some time on your part, and to get the most out of it you should create a marketing launch (for more information on launches, check out Jeff Walker's book, "Launch"). This is not a set-it-and-forget-it type of thing.

By the time you get to this point in The Funnel Philosophy you should already have a loyal, dedicated tribe of raving fans but you will still have to show them the value this product brings to their life, and that you are the right person to deliver it.

As a general rule, I like to conduct one big launch per quarter. This allows you to keep adding massive amounts of value to your audience without constantly asking for the sale. Continue to produce high-value weekly podcasts, and then for one or two weeks each quarter, go through a Jeff Walker-style product launch.

Now you've drastically increase your income, and with well-executed product launches you will have some big paydays. In our last section of The Funnel Philosophy, we will take a look at how to truly maximize your income.

HIGH-PRICED SUBSCRIPTION

This is like adding rocket fuel to your business. We talked earlier in The Funnel Philosophy about the benefit of the recurring income from low-priced subscriptions, now image the impact of a $1,000-plus-per-month subscription!

Make no mistake, in order to offer a high-priced subscription it's going to take a lot of time and energy on your part. You will need to deliver amazing value. In fact, the most popular way I see people conducting high-priced subscriptions is through live mastermind groups. The value of getting a group of high-level business owners in the same room to focus on helping each other solve problems is amazing and is often worth ten to twenty times the price of the monthly subscription cost.

This is a funnel level that most business owners do not get to. You shouldn't attempt it until you know you can deliver an outstanding return for all of your clients. If you can't deliver on that promise you will do an incredible amount of damage to your brand and your reputation, so proceed with caution.

Once, you get to this level of The Funnel Philosophy the sky's the limit. You are now maximizing your impact and your income.

PowerOfPodcastingBook.com

LAUNCHING YOUR PODCAST

Lots of people give advice on "how to take advantage of iTunes New & Noteworthy" and in just a bit I will throw my recommendations into the ring, but before I do I need to say, ***STOP CARRYING ABOUT NEW AND NOTEWORTHY!!!***

At most this is 56 days of your podcasting journey, so you NEED to look well beyond 56 days if you have any hopes of using podcasts to grow your business. Yes, New and Noteworthy can help give you a boost in listeners however, it is significantly more important that you create a solid structure for your podcast and set the right expectations. You are trying to build a habit, and the expectation from your audience is that you deliver value on a consistent regular, predictable basis. If you are running some crazy launch strategy you will likely only confuse your listeners. Also, if you try to be too ambitious, especially if this is your first show, there is a good chance you will burn out or outrun yourself. You are better off to release only one episode per week at the same day and time, and slowly grow your audience naturally.

Now after that warning, if you are ready to take advantage of the potentially massive iTunes New and Noteworthy audience, here is a plan that will get you good results:

Three weeks out: At this point you should have three episodes recorded and ideally ready or mostly ready to go, with plans to record a few more that week. Set up a "Podcast coming soon page". This can be very simple or a more detailed page to explain the premise of the podcast and give listeners an idea of what to expect. The essential element is an email opt-in form so they can be notified when the podcast is live. If you have an existing email list I would let those customers also know you have a podcast coming soon.

Two weeks out: Make a few announcements on social media that you have a podcast coming soon. Take a one- or two-minute clip (make sure it's a good, engaging moment) and create it as a trailer for your soon-to-be-launched podcast. Send the trailer to your email list and post it on social media. This is when I also create the behind-the-scenes elements for review giveaway contests that run the first two weeks the podcast is live.

One week out: Submit your podcast to iTunes. iTunes can take up to a week to approve podcasts. If you are brand new and not sure you are setting up things right you might even want to submit it earlier. Lately, iTunes has been approving the shows I've submitted much quicker than before. The last four have been approved in less than 24 hours. Some of you will be tempted to wait to submit your podcast so you can squeak out every possible day from the 56 New and Noteworthy limit. This is a bad idea. One, there is the chance your approval will take longer. Two, you want to have some time after it is approved before you announce it to the world. This is the time to call your friends, family, business associates, cats, and dogs to leave a review on iTunes. You want to pre-populate your podcast with reviews from those close to you so when you do announce it to the public, at least a handful of reviews are already posted. This will help encourage people not only to subscribe and listen but also to leave a review themselves.

During these first eight weeks, reviews are your lifeblood. They will boost your ranking more than anything else. Go as far as sending individual emails with instructions on how to submit a review, or walking people you are with through the process. Every review helps.

Launch Day: It's finally time to take your podcast live! When you announce your show to the world there should be three episodes available. Not one, not twenty — three. The reason you want multiple episode is because that will allow your listeners to get a better feel for the show.

They will likely be excited and listen to all three right away. This will give you a big boost on iTunes as well, since the recency of listens and upload play a factor in your ranking. There are three specific episodes that I have every client create for those initial episodes. The first is an introductory episode. This should give an overview of who you are, why you created the podcast, and what to expect moving forward. It is important to have this episode. Many people who stumble onto your show will go back and listen to this episode, hoping to get an idea of who you are and what you are all about. In almost every single podcast I run, the first episode is the one listened to the most.

In the second episode it's time to focus on you delivering content. Remember, for this podcast to really grow your business, you need to be seen as an expert. Even if you will be interviewing guests on a regular basis you need to be able to deliver the value on your own or with a co-host. This second episode is the first time for you to show your stuff. Do some teaching, offer some lessons, or share a compelling case study. Make it clear that you are not just another person who interviews people. You also have the skills to back it up.

The third episode should be an interview with a great guest. Ideally, interview someone who has a little bit of an audience and is willing to share the episode with their audience. This helps you get noticed by a new group of people.

On launch day you will want to announce a review contest. Holding some sort of contest to help gather reviews for your podcast is a great idea. Examples of prizes include books, video courses, coaching packages, or products that relate to your topic (i.e. If it's a fitness podcast, you could give away a Vitamix blender). One thing I would caution against: items like iPads, Bose headphones, etc. are great prizes that will get you lots of reviews. The problem is a lot of those reviews will be from people who only want to leave a review for the chance to win the big prizes. They have no real affinity for you or your message, and they won't be listeners. I believe it's important to cater to your true fans — people who believe in you, your message, and your podcast.

That's why giving away your products or items that closely align to your brand and message is the way to go. You are still offering to give away something of value, but it's extra valuable to someone who is already a fan and tribe member.

The final thing for you to do on launch day is to spread the news out far and wide. Send an email to your list, post about it on all social media accounts, tell people you know to share it, and even individually email people. If you start getting positive feedback right away, or use a previously posted review, you can share that on social media as a way to have multiple updates without seeming extra annoying.

After Launch Day: After launch day and during those first 56 days while you are in New and Noteworthy, there are a few things you can do to give yourself an extra boost to stay ranked high in this section. Again, the main thing to focus on during this whole time is reviews. Reviews, reviews, reviews. You might want to create a video explaining to people exactly how to subscribe to a podcast and leave a review (See

YourPodcastGuru.com/BookResources for an example). You will want to make that your one and only CTA for at least the first few weeks at the end of the podcast.

Make sure to maintain a consistent podcast schedule. Tell people what day they can expect a new episode each week and deliver a new episode ON THAT DAY. It sounds simple, but if you don't do this, you will ruin the momentum you are gaining from podcasting. If podcasting is purely a hobby for you, then release an episode when you feel like it. If it's a tool to grow your business, stick to a consistent schedule.

Many podcasters will release extra episodes during their first few weeks as a way to boost rankings. This practice works and is a good strategy to use. I recommend a couple tweaks. At minimum, make it clear to your listeners from the get-go that the extra episodes each week will only happen for a short time. The last thing you want is for people to be upset when you cut back on episodes or think the podcast isn't popular enough to warrant a schedule of multiple episodes per week. A great way around this issue is to release clearly marked bonus episodes. These could be shorter-form episodes or episodes that are in a unique format, or, in the intro section, you could simply say it is an extra bonus for listeners. Don't rely on text to communicate this. You need to state it in the audio.

A great example of this strategy is how we launched the DREAM.THINK.DO. Podcast. Mitch, the host of the show, conducted some great interviews with people about the dream careers they had built for themselves. This was great content that was along the same lines of the DREAM.THINIK.DO. Podcast, but not an exact fit. So, we decided to release those earlier in the week as bonus episodes. We used the DREAM.THINK.DO intro bumper, Mitch recorded a special section introducing the interview and saying that this was a bonus episode, then we played the originally recorded interview and ended with the DREAM.THINK.DO outro bumper. Something like this is a great way to provide more value to your listeners, boost your rankings in iTunes, and not risk damaging your credibility when the bonus episodes stop.

GAINING MORE LISTENERS

The main focus of almost every podcaster I've ever met is to gain more listeners, to grow the podcast. There are obvious reasons that increasing your number of downloads has a strong appeal, but before we go into strategies on how to do that, I have a word of caution. Getting a large number of listeners is NOT a good goal. Ultimately, your podcast needs to have quality listeners who turn into customers, so it's less important to have many listeners than it is to have the right listeners.

Not only that, but we can often discount the value of the people listening. Say your podcast gets 100 downloads on each weekly episode. That might not seem like a lot and sometimes podcasters will get upset about that. But think of it this way, how often do you get the chance to speak in front of 100 people? With your podcast, you are getting to speak to the same 100 people every week! That's a big relationship builder and extremely powerful. So don't let the stats distract you from what's behind them: real people listening to your message.

Raving Fans

The best way to gain more listeners is to turn your current listeners into raving fans. At least a subset of your audience should love what you do and want to promote it to the world. This takes some time to cultivate, but once you begin to create those true fans your business will take off.

Creating raving fans is actually simpler than you might think. There are only a few elements needed:

Authenticity: I know the word "authentic" is thrown around a lot, but that isn't without good reason. In order to create raving fans people need to connect with your voice. They need to know your style and your personality; they should be able to see or hear something and be able to know how they think you would react to that. Let your quirks, and eccentricities shine through. Don't try to hide them and fit in like everyone else. You will be lost in the shuffle. To create raving fans you will need to stand out. That can be scary or intimidating I know, but the only way to create a real audience is to be uniquely you no matter what.

Add value: That's what this whole book is about. Adding value to your audience consistently will help your business grow. Look for ways to add value at every opportunity. That does not mean you should give everything away for free. In fact, if you do that you are actually taking away value from your audience. It means that you should look for ways to help them solve a problem, look for ways to connect with them, and look for ways to entertain them. Without the value piece, people will not care about you.

Be Consistent: Consistency is key. People need to trust you. One of the best ways to build that trust is to show up again and again on a predictable basis. That's why I believe your podcast needs to release every week on the same day and time. It's a small act that allows people to trust you. It removes another barrier for them.

How many raving fans do you have right now? One way to gauge that in your mind is to think, "if I launched a new product right now that met one of the major needs in my audience, who can I count on to buy it? Or if I asked an important question to my audience, who can I count on to respond?" Your raving fans will show up for you when you need them. They will do what it takes to stay engaged and involved in the work you do. Once you being to figure out who those people are, go the extra mile to make sure they feel appreciated. Time spent with your raving fans will pay off in spades.

CREATING ENGAGEMENT

Creating engagement with your audience can drastically enhance your podcast. It will help your audience develop a stronger relationship with you. They will have more buy-in with your show and start to see it more as a community instead of just a place to get information.

There are a few ways you can work to increase audience engagement. We mentioned a couple of strategies that will help with this, but in this section I'll cover a few more.

One great way is to answer listener questions. Once you have started to receive emails or messages from people asking for your advice, you can consider adding a special segment or even an entire episode to your podcast in which you focus on answering listener questions. I recommend using a service like SpeakPipe for people who call in with their question. This gives people a chance to hear their voices on your show and makes the podcast feel more interactive even for those listeners who never call.

Another great way to create engagement with listeners is to do a live show. This could be a separate, special live show in addition to your regular episodes — the "Mac Power Users" podcast does a great job of this with its live feedback show. Another option is to always record your show at a set time with a chat room or with comments open to the public. "Self Publishing Podcast" does this each week through Google Hangouts. This allows them to interact with and answer questions from some of their most dedicated listeners throughout the show.

ENGAGING WITH NEW LISTENERS

Driving traffic to your podcast is more important than ever, especially after your magical eight-week New & Noteworthy period. In this section I'll cover a few of the emerging ways to drive traffic and convert your listeners into customers, which is the ultimate goal of your show.

I won't go into too much detail because I do not feel I've had enough of a chance to test them. But these are a few areas I am exploring with my clients and we are seeing some early results. My recommendation: test. A few of the strategies on this list require a little time and money, but can return significant results. Try those out right away and then dip your toe in with the rest to see if they make sense and get the results you wanted.

> **Images:** This was briefly touched on in the branding section of the book, but having specific engaging episode art is one of the best ways to increase the number of social media shares you receive. Spend some time and even consider hiring a graphic designer to create

images for you. At Your Podcast Guru we work with a team of designers to create a unique and consistent brand image for each podcast. This is one thing that sets our shows apart from others.

Multiple Social Media Posts: Social media feeds move fast, and in platforms that curate your content, like Facebook, only a small percentage of your audience sees your post. That's when posting about your new episode a couple of times on release day and the following day is very helpful. I recommend using different types of posts, one focusing on an image with the episode title and another focusing on an important quotation and a link for example.

Another important thing to think about in regards to social media is to recycle your old episodes. If your podcast is on Episode 74, many of your social media followers likely have never heard Episode 8. Episode 8 is still valuable and useful to them, they have just never been exposed to it. One tool that has been a game-changer with this is Edgar. Edgar

(YourPodcastGuru.com/Edgar) allows you to create categories of social media posts that continually re-cycle and post without you have to re-upload content. I use it with every client, and we are seeing great results.

Video Teaser Trailers: Getting earballs on your podcast can be difficult. A way to increase your audience that I believe will be more popular in the future is through quality video trailers. With this, think movie trailer. At the simplest level, take 30 to 90 seconds of an interview or a segment you think would really entice your ideal audience to want to listen to the podcast. You would turn that segment into a video that pushes people to your audio podcast. The video is uploaded to YouTube and directly to Facebook. The YouTube video can also be shared across several different social media channels. Quick, behind-the-scenes recordings for Instagram and Twitter also could give you some more traffic if done correctly.

One-Sheet Guides: If you want a great way to increase the number of people who opt-in to your email list, offer some unique resource guides, or one-sheets, that go along with a specific episode. This should be something that is easy to consume. A one-page resource guide of recommended tools, a quick outline guide to what you covered in the episode, or a checklist are all great examples. Once you create this one-sheet, use a service like Leadpages to have an opt-in form in your show notes for that episode.

SMS Opt-In: Podcasts are great for expanding your audience, but real sales happen in your email list. The problem with turning podcast listeners into email list subscribers is that the listeners are usually on the go, and typing in the traditional URL is simply too much work to do from your phone. But sending a text message is easy. Many services are now popping up to allow you to capture subscribers to your email list through text message. You will see more podcasts with this option. For even better results, combine SMS opt-in with a unique one-sheet.

Autoresponders: Autoresponders are like

magic. They allow you to create a message once, put it in the exact sequence, and deliver that message at the appropriate time to your clients lifecycle within your business. This is a powerful tool when used correctly. I think it is just beginning to be used by podcasters and we will see it become more widespread soon. Imagine someone finds your podcast on Episode 111, and joins your email list. You could have an autoresponder set up to introduce them to you, give them highlights of your most popular episodes, and get them up to speed and engaged with your show automatically. After a handful of value-focused emails you will have built enough reciprocity to sell some of your products or services. Combine autoresponders with unique one-sheets and SMS opt-ins and you have a game-changing strategy.

Podcasting will continue to evolve. Yes, it is an older form of internet media, having been around since 2005, but it wasn't until the proliferation of the smartphone that podcasting began to really grow in popularity. It's only within the last couple years that the mass market has even been aware of podcasting. This platform and the businesses that use it will quickly find new ways to engage and interact with their audiences.

THE FUTURE OF PODCASTS

Will podcasts disappear?

Audio content will be here for a long time. Radio survived TV, and audio content will continue to live on in some form for many, many years. Audio will always be a coveted format because it is so easy to consume. It requires no screen time, and you can consume it while doing other tasks like working out or driving.

Yes, podcasting will evolve and change. It already is changing rapidly, but you will never go wrong producing content to which your audience can listen.

Is podcasting fading? No, but we are in a podcasting bubble. Podcasting is trendy. New podcasts are being created constantly, and it is constantly getting harder and harder to see results from a podcast. Back in the early days you could record audio on a conference call line and expect to see great results. That's no longer the case. Being top on New & Noteworthy used to mean you could expect 10,000's of listeners, now it's closer to 1,000's.

But this bubble is a good thing.

As more and more people jump into creating podcasts they will bring swarms of new podcast listeners, people who will find your show appealing. Soon this bubble will burst. People will demand more from their listening experiences. The masses will want radio-quality broadcasts that deliver their content in a professional, educational, or entertaining way. This means that many podcasts won't survive. They won't be able to keep up with the quality needed to rise to the top, leading to fewer, higher-quality podcasts to reap the rewards.

The other major reason you need to pay attention to podcasting — it's about to hit mainstream. There are a few things that have happened over the last year that have put podcasting in the perfect position to gain massive amounts of listeners. First, is the quality and mass appeal of podcasts. Shows like "Serial", "Startup", and others are making their way into the news, and podcasts are now referenced in TV and movies.

It is easier than ever to subscribe to podcasts. With the release of iOS 8 the Podcast app can't be removed from iPhones and iPads, meaning more people will at least be curious about what that purple app on their phone does. Podcasts are the No. 1 reason people visit the iTunes store, so Apple will likely keep investing because more people on the iTunes store means more sales.

In 2015, listening to podcasts on the road just got a whole lot easier. Before, you would need to figure out a way to connect your phone through your speakers and had to play the podcasts that were downloaded or streamed on your phone. Now, every 2015 model vehicle is rolling off the lot with the ability to subscribe and listen to podcasts from the dashboard. AM or FM radio are no longer your only options, now you can find the podcast content that is perfect for you. This opens up a new sea of potential listeners for your show.

The Power of Podcasting

APPENDIX

Here is a list of my recommended resources. No, you do not need everything in this list to get started podcasting. However, I do recommend you make some investment in your show. Have the best audio quality that you can.

Microphones

>**ATR2100:** This is a very versatile dynamic microphone. It has both USB and XLR connections, making it a great starting microphone that will allow you to slowly upgrade.
>
>YourPodcastGuru.com/ATR2100

Hell PR40: This is the premium podcast mic. If you are looking for the highest quality and best sound, go with this one.

YourPodcastGuru.com/Heil

BoomStand: This boom arm is designed for the Heil but you can use it for the ATR2100 as well. Make sure your mic is always in the right position with this.

YourPodcastGuru.com/BoomStand

Shock Mount: This helps prevent noise from moving the mic or bumping the table. Use if you have the Heil.

YourPodcastGuru.com/ShockMount

Pop Filter: This helps prevent those plosives (where your "p" make a popping sound) from happening. Another must if you have the Heil.

YourPodcastGuru.com/PopFilter

The Power of Podcasting

Rode SmartLav: Podcasting on the go, recording a speech, or video podcasting? This is the best sounding lavaliere that I've found.

YourPodcastGuru.com/SmartLav

Hardware

Roland R-05: Great for field recording and as an external recorder. I don't like to record audio directly to my computer. This is what I use and recommend for capturing all your audio.

YourPodcastGuru.com/Roland

Behringer 802 Mixer: Once you move up to a microphone like the Heil PR40, you are going to want a mixer. This great starter mixer. It allows you to record audio from up to eight different channels.

YourPodcastGuru.com/802

Mackie Mixer: This is the premium-level mixer. When you are ready to step up to higher quality, go with the Mackie. I recommend getting an eight-channel mixer.

YourPodcastGuru.com/Mackie

iMic: Do you need to connect your mixer to your computer in order to run Skype interviews? This adapter is your answer.

YourPodcastGuru.com/imic

Mic Flag: Add that extra element of professionalism to your studio by getting your business or podcast logo printed on a mic flag. This flag works great with the Heil boom stand and either the Heil PR40 or ATR2100.

YourPodcastGuru.com/micflag

Logitech Pro C920 webcam: If you are recording video on your Skype interviews, I highly recommend going with this camera instead of the built-in camera. You will get a much cleaner, clearer picture.

The Power of Podcasting

YourPodcastGuru.com/webcam

Sony Headphones: These headphones are the ones used by many radio stations; they will give you the truest sound to help you monitor your recording process.

YourPodcastGuru.com/headphones

Software:

eCamm Call Recorder for Skype: If you need a simple way to record Skype interviews, this is the best program out there.

YourPodcastGuru.com/CallRecorder

Adobe Audition: Edit your podcast audio like a pro. This is the only program I recommend.
YourPodcastGuru.com/audition

Screenflow: This is the best software for capturing and editing screen recordings. I am amazed at how much I use this program; it is good for everything from videos on how to subscribe to a podcast, to content for my audience to instructions for my team.

YourPodcastGuru.com/screenflow

1Password: While this program is not directly related to podcast, too many people have poor online security habits. 1Password solves that problem plus it makes it ridiculously easy to log in to websites.

YourPodcastGuru.com/OnePassword

Additional Podcast Resources

SpeakPipe: Are you looking to play audio questions from you audience on the podcast? Or do you like to give people the ability to leave a quick testimonial that you could use during your show? SpeakPipe serves as a

The Power of Podcasting

voicemail box that sends you an MP3 file you can mix directly into a podcast episode. I love this service.

YourPodcastGuru.com/SpeakPipe

Audiojungle: This is where I purchase almost all of my stock audio sounds. They have a large library that is constantly being updated, is easily categorized, and very reasonable priced. It is the perfect spot to find your theme song.

YourPodcastGuru.com/Audiojungle

Make My Intro: Tim is the voice behind many of the top podcasts' intros. He will help you create the perfect intro for your show. I've used Tim for a few projects. If you end up using him, just mention that you heard about him from me.

YourPodcastGuru.com/MakeMyIntro

MusicRadioCreative: This is a very high-quality service. From script writing to original audio sounds to finding the right voice talent for your intro and audio segments. If you want your podcast to really stand out, check out Music Radio Creative.

YourPodcastGuru.com/MusicRadioCreative

Canva: As mentioned in this book, the way your podcast looks is important. If you are doing the artwork yourself I highly recommend Canva. It gives you a great foundation. Stick to one or two layout styles to give your podcast a consistent feel.

YourPodcastGuru.com/Canva

Bluehost: I'm a big believer that your business needs to be run on a self-hosted Wordpress website. I use Bluehost for all my hosting needs.

YourPodcastGuru.com/Bluehost

Powerpress: This is the plugin that helps me run all of my podcasts. I use it to generate the RSS feeds, and manage the podcast.

The Power of Podcasting

YourPodcastGuru.com/Powerpress

Pretty Links: Most people listen to podcasts on the go, or while doing another activity. When mentioning resources or calls to action, it's important to make them easy and memorable for your listeners. That's where Pretty Links comes it. It takes a long and difficult URL and turns it into a short, simple link. All the resource links in this book were created with Pretty Link.

YourPodcastGuru.com/PrettyLinks

Libsyn: Your podcast audio NEEDS to be hosted somewhere other than your Wordpress website. There are only two services I recommend, and Libsyn is by far the simplest, and has the longest track record of the two.

YourPodcastGuru.com/Libsyn

Aweber: The No. 1 job of your podcast is to help your email list grow. Your email list is still the most valuable asset you have as a business owner. Aweber is the emailing service I recommend. I love its functionality, and once you start diving into autoresponders, it will feel like magic. I've built and developed two business on the back of this service.

YourPodcastGuru.com/Aweber

Leadpages: Landing, sales, and opt-in pages are essential to running your online business, but they can be a little tricky to get right. Leadpages makes that easy. You can have these pages up and running in five minutes and they will be fully integrated with your email service. This service is a game-changer.

YourPodcastGuru.com/Leadpages

Elegant Themes: You want your website to look good, but I see way too many people get hung up on creating a website design that is completely customized. That is a waste of your time at the beginning. Find a good solid, premium paid Wordpress theme, customize it with your graphics and color choices, and GET BACK TO BUSINESS. Elegant Themes is my favorite theme resource.

The Power of Podcasting

YourPodcastGuru.com/ElegantThemes

Shutterstock: Visuals are essential to good content these days. I love Shutterstock. It's where I get all my stock images.

YourPodcastGuru.com/Shutterstock

Special FREE Bonus Gift for You

To help you to achieve more success in your business, there are **FREE BONUS RESOURCES** for you at:

FreeGiftFromNick.com

- Three in depth videos on how to grow your business through content creation, and re-purposing
- Downloadable "Roadmap to Podcasting" Resource Guide

Don't wait start maximizing your impact and income with these free gifts!!

FreeGiftFromNick.com

Additional Resources

Are you looking to deliver value to your audience every week with next to no effort? Check out one of the podcasting services below from Your Podcast Guru to learn how you can maximize your impact and income without all the hassle.

Basic Podcasting Package

This package will get you a weekly podcast. All you have to do is send in the audio and we take care of the rest. From editing to show notes to emailing your list to even posting on social media.

This package includes:
- Onboarding Process to get you ready to launch
- Basic Studio Equipment (ATR2100, boomstand)
- Branding Asset Development
- Editing, and publishing weekly podcast episodes
- Podcast Email List Creation and Curation

YourPodcastGuru.com/Services

Premium Podcasting Package

This package takes what the Basic Podcasting package offers and cranks it up. This package is designed to grow you audience and business in a big way.

This package includes:
- Recording studio upgrade (Heil PR40, Boomstand, Mixer, Recorder)
- 1 Teaser Trailer Video per month
- 1 One-Sheet per month
- 1 Autoresponder Email per month
- SMS (text message) Opt-ind Curation

YourPodcastGuru.com/Services

ABOUT NICK

Nick Palkowski is the owner of Your Podcast Guru, a business that is helping you get your message to your audience in order to increase your impact and income.

Nick started Your Podcast Guru in May 2014 to help speakers and business owners grow their business by providing a podcasting service that allows his clients to focus on creating amazing content while Your Podcast Guru takes care of all the rest.

From launching a podcast to growing your email list to setting up your sales funnel, Your Podcast Guru helps the strategy and execution of all the steps you need.

YourPodcastGuru.com

Made in the USA
Middletown, DE
08 November 2015